all abc Cotton

MW01049634

Soft and cool yet sturdy and durable, cotton yarn is perfect for crochet projects to use in the kitchen, bath, and all through the home.

6

25

28

LEISURE ARTS, INC. • Maumelle, Arkansas

 EASY

SHOPPING LIST

Yarn (Medium Weight) 

[2.8 ounces, 140 yards (80 grams, 128 meters) per skein]:

- ☐ Main Color - 1{2-4} skein(s)
- ☐ Contrasting Color - 1 skein

Crochet Hook

- ☐ Size H (5 mm) **or** size needed for gauge

SIZE INFORMATION

Size: Small{Medium-Large}

Finished Bottom:

6{8¼-12}" long x 4{4¾-6}" wide/

15{21-30.5} cm x 10{12-15} cm

Finished Height:

4¾{6-8¾}"/12{15-22} cm

(before edging or folding on Size Large)

Size Note: We have printed the instructions for the sizes in different colors to make it easier for you to find:

- Size Small in Blue
- Size Medium in Pink
- Size Large in Green

Instructions in Black apply to all sizes.

GAUGE INFORMATION

13 sc and 12 rows/rnds = 4" (10 cm)

Gauge Swatch: 4" (10 cm) square

Holding 2 strands of Main Color together, ch 14.

Row 1: Sc in second ch from hook and in each ch across: 13 sc.

Rows 2-12: Ch 1, turn; sc in each sc across.

Finish off.

Oval Baskets

BOTTOM

Holding 2 strands of Main Color together, ch 9{15-22}.

Rnd 1 (Right side)**:** Sc in second ch from hook and in each ch across to last ch, 3 sc in last ch; working in free loops of beginning ch ***(Fig. 2b, page 30)***, sc in next 6{12-19} chs, 2 sc in next ch; join with slip st to first sc: 18{30-44} sc.

Note: Loop a short piece of yarn around any stitch to mark Rnd 1 as **right** side.

Rnd 2: Ch 1, sc in same st as joining and in next 7{13-20} sc, 3 sc in next sc, sc in next 8{14-21} sc, 3 sc in last sc; join with slip st to first sc: 22{34-48} sc.

Rnd 3: Ch 1, sc in same st as joining and in next 7{13-20} sc, 2 sc in next sc, sc in next sc, 2 sc in next sc, sc in next 8{14-21} sc, 2 sc in next sc, sc in next sc, 2 sc in last sc; join with slip st to first sc: 26{38-52} sc.

Rnd 4: Ch 1, sc in same st as joining and in next 6{12-19} sc, 2 sc in next sc, (sc in next sc, 2 sc in next sc) 3 times, sc in next 6{12-19} sc, 2 sc in next sc, (sc in next sc, 2 sc in next sc) twice, sc in last sc and in same sc as first sc; join with slip st to first sc: 34{46-60} sc.

Rnd 5: Ch 1, sc in same st as joining and in next 7{13-20} sc, 2 sc in next sc, sc in next 7 sc, 2 sc in next sc, sc in next 8{14-21} sc, 2 sc in next sc, sc in next 7 sc, 2 sc in last sc; join with slip st to first sc: 38{50-64} sc.

SIZE SMALL ONLY

Rnd 6: Ch 1, sc in same st as joining and in next 8 sc, 2 sc in next sc, (sc in next 3 sc, 2 sc in next sc) twice, sc in next 10 sc, 2 sc in next sc, (sc in next 3 sc, 2 sc in next sc) twice, sc in last sc: join with slip st to Back Loop Only of first sc ***(Fig. 3, page 30)***: 44 sc.

SIZES MEDIUM & LARGE ONLY

Rnd 6: Ch 1, sc in same st as joining and in next {14-21} sc, 2 sc in next sc, (sc in next 3 sc, 2 sc in next sc) twice, sc in next {16-23} sc, 2 sc in next sc, (sc in next 3 sc, 2 sc in next sc) twice, sc in last sc; join with slip st to first sc: {56-70} sc.

SIZE MEDIUM ONLY

Rnd 7: Ch 1, sc in same st as joining and in next 15 sc, 2 sc in next sc, sc in next 9 sc, 2 sc in next sc, sc in next 17 sc, 2 sc in next sc, sc in next 9 sc, 2 sc in next sc, sc in last sc; join with slip st to Back Loop Only of first sc ***(Fig. 3, page 30)***: 60 sc.

SIZE LARGE ONLY

Rnd 7: Ch 1, sc in same st as joining and in next 22 sc, 2 sc in next sc, (sc in next 4 sc, 2 sc in next sc) twice, sc in next 24 sc, 2 sc in next sc, (sc in next 4 sc, 2 sc in next sc) twice, sc in last sc; join with slip st to first sc: 76 sc.

Rnd 8: Ch 1, sc in same st as joining and in next 23 sc, 2 sc in next sc, sc in next 3 sc, 2 sc in next sc, sc in next 2 sc, 2 sc in next sc, sc in next 3 sc, 2 sc in next sc, sc in next 26 sc, 2 sc in next sc, sc in next 3 sc, 2 sc in next sc, sc in next 2 sc, 2 sc in next sc, sc in next 3 sc, 2 sc in next sc, sc in last 2 sc; join with slip st to first sc: 84 sc.

Rnd 9: Ch 1, sc in same st as joining and in each sc around; join with slip st to Back Loop Only of first sc ***(Fig. 3, page 30)***.

SIDES (All Sizes)

Rnd 1: Ch 1, sc in Back Loop Only of same st as joining and each sc around; join with slip st to **both** loops of first sc: 44{60-84} sc.

Rnds 2 thru 14{18-26}: Ch 1, sc in both loops of same st as joining and each sc around; join with slip st to first sc.

Finish off.

TRIM

Add one of the following trims to any size basket.

FRINGE

Holding 3 strands of Contrasting Color together, each 10" (25.5 cm) long, add fringe in every other sc on last rnd *(Figs. A & B)*.

Fig. A

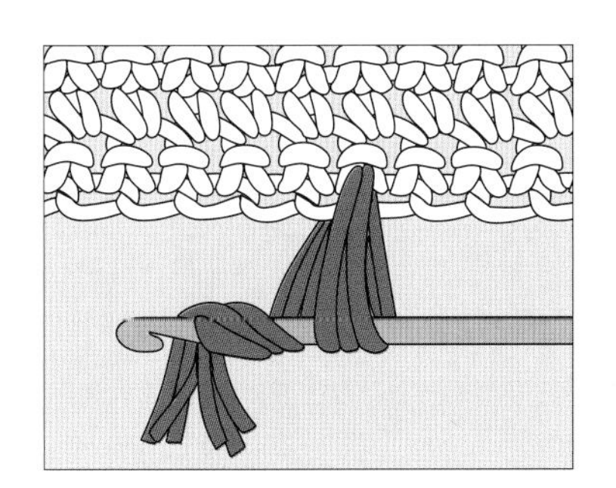

Fig. B

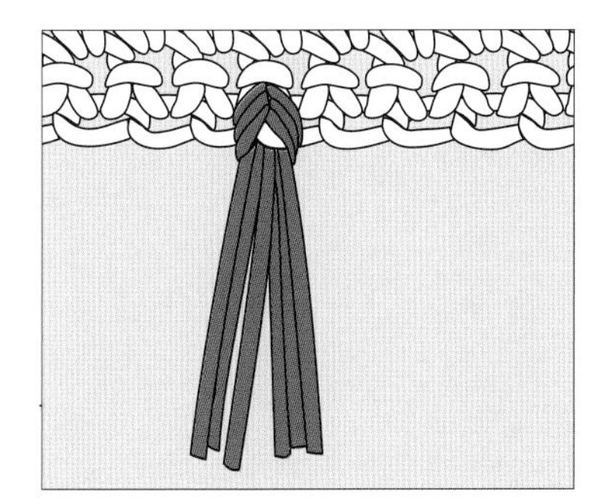

SHELL EDGING

Rnd 1: With **right** side facing, join one strand of Contrasting Color with sc in any sc on last rnd ***(see Joining With Sc, page 30)***; sc in each sc around; join with slip st to first sc: 44{60-84} sc.

Rnd 2: Ch 1, sc in same st as joining, skip next sc, 5 dc in next sc, skip next sc, ★ sc in next sc, skip next sc, 5 dc in next sc, skip next sc; repeat from ★ around; join with slip st to first sc, finish off.

LONG SC EDGING

To work Long sc *(abbreviated LSC)*, working **around** previous rnd, insert hook in sc indicated ***(Fig. C)***, YO and pull up a loop even with last st made, YO and draw through both loops on hook.

Fig. C

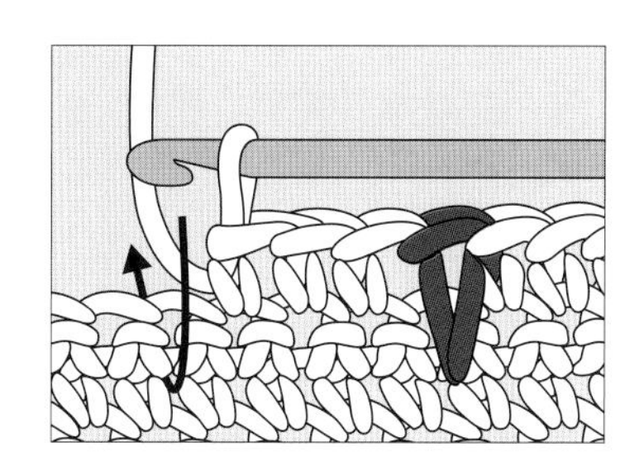

Rnd 1: With **right** side facing, join 2 strands of Contrasting Color with sc in any sc on last rnd ***(see Joining With Sc, page 30)***; sc in next 2 sc, work LSC in sc one rnd **below** next sc, ★ sc in next 3 sc, work LSC in sc one rnd **below** next sc; repeat from ★ around; join with slip st to first sc, finish off.

Designs by Marly Bird.

Bottle Carrier

 EASY

Finished Size: Fits an 8" (20.5 cm) 16.9 fluid ounce bottle

SHOPPING LIST

Yarn (Medium Weight) 
[2.1 ounces, 105 yards (60 grams, 96 meters) per skein]:
- ☐ 1 skein

Crochet Hook
- ☐ Size H (5 mm) **or** size needed for gauge

Additional Supplies
- ☐ Yarn needle

GAUGE INFORMATION

13 dc = 4" (10 cm)
Gauge Swatch: 3¼" (8.25 cm) diameter
Work same as Bottom.

STITCH GUIDE

PICOT
Ch 3, sc in third ch from hook.

BOTTOM

Rnd 1 (Right side)**:** Make an adjustable loop to form a ring ***(Figs. 1a-d, page 30)***; ch 2, 9 dc in ring; join with slip st to top of beginning ch: 10 sts.

Note: Loop a short piece of yarn around any stitch to mark Rnd 1 as **right** side.

Rnd 2: Ch 3 **(counts as first dc, now and throughout)**, dc in same st as joining, 2 dc in next dc and in each dc around; join with slip st to first dc: 20 dc.

Rnd 3: Ch 3, dc in same st as joining and in next 4 dc, (2 dc in next dc, dc in next 4 dc) around; join with slip st to first dc: 24 dc.

SIDES

Rnd 1: Ch 3, dc in next dc and in each dc around; join with slip st to first dc.

Rnd 2: Ch 1, sc in same st as joining, work Picot, skip next dc, (sc in next dc, work Picot, skip next dc) around; join with slip st to first sc: 12 sc.

Rnd 3: Ch 1, sc in same st as joining, (ch 4, skip next Picot, sc in next sc) around to last Picot, ch 1, skip last Picot, dc in first sc to form last ch-4 sp: 12 ch-4 sps.

Rnd 4: Ch 1, sc in last ch-4 sp made, work Picot, (sc in next ch-4 sp, work Picot) around; join with slip st to first sc: 12 sc.

Rnds 5-14: Repeat Rnds 3 and 4, 5 times: 12 sc.

Rnd 15: Ch 3, dc in same st as joining, 2 dc in each sc around skipping Picots; join with slip st to first dc: 24 dc.

Rnd 16: Ch 1, (slip st in next dc, ch 1) around; join with slip st to joining slip st; finish off leaving a long end for sewing.

STRAP

Ch 100.

Row 1 (Right side)**:** Hdc in third ch from hook **(2 skipped chs count as first hdc)** and in each ch across: 99 hdc.

Note: Mark Row 1 as **right** side.

Rows 2 and 3: Ch 1 **(does not count as a st)**, turn; hdc in each hdc across.

Trim: Ch 1, do **not** turn; (slip st, ch 1) evenly around entire Strap ***(Fig. 2b, page 30)***; join with slip st to first st, finish off leaving a long end for sewing.

Sew ends of Strap to outside of Carrier.

Design by Cathy Hardy.

Lacy Tote

 EASY

Finished Size: 15" wide (Bottom Section) x 19" high (38 cm x 48.5 cm) (excluding strap)

SHOPPING LIST

Yarn (Medium Weight) MEDIUM 4

[2.8 ounces, 140 yards
(80 grams, 128 meters) per skein]:

- ☐ Color A (Green) - 2 skeins
- ☐ Color B (White) - 1 skein

[2.1 ounces, 105 yards
(60 grams, 96 meters) per skein]:

- ☐ Color C (Variegated) - 2 skeins

Crochet Hook

- ☐ Size H (5 mm)
  or size needed for gauge

Additional Supplies

- ☐ Yarn needle

GAUGE INFORMATION

13 dc = 4" (10 cm),
In Bottom Section pattern,
3 dc groups and 8 rnds = 4" (10 cm)

Gauge Swatch: 4" wide (10 cm)
With Color A, ch 15.
Row 1: Dc in fourth ch from hook **(3 skipped chs count as first dc)** and in each ch across: 13 dc.
Rows 2-4: Ch 3 **(counts as first dc)**, turn; dc in next dc and in each dc across.
Finish off.

STITCH GUIDE

PICOT
Ch 3, sc in third ch from hook.

BOTTOM SECTION

With Color A, ch 39.

Rnd 1 (Right side)**:** 5 Dc in fourth ch from hook **(3 skipped chs count as first dc)**, dc in next ch and in each ch across to last ch, 6 dc in last ch; working in free loops of beginning ch ***(Fig. 2b, page 30)***, dc in next 34 chs; join with slip st to first dc: 80 dc.

Note: Loop a short piece of yarn around any stitch to mark Rnd 1 as **right** side.

Rnd 2: Ch 3 **(counts as first dc, now and throughout)**, dc in same st as joining, † dc in next dc, 2 dc in each of next 2 dc, dc in next dc, 2 dc in next dc, dc in next 34 dc †, 2 dc in next dc, repeat from † to † once; join with slip st to first dc: 88 dc.

Rnd 3: Ch 3, (dc, work Picot, 2 dc) in same st as joining, ★ ch 1, skip next 3 dc, (2 dc, work Picot, 2 dc) in next dc; repeat from ★ around to last 3 dc, skip last 3 dc, sc in first dc to form last ch-1 sp: 22 groups and 22 ch-1 sps.

Rnd 4: Ch 1, sc in last ch-1 sp made, ch 6, (sc in next ch-1 sp, ch 6) around; join with slip st to first sc: 22 ch-6 sps.

Rnd 5: Slip st in first ch-6 sp, ch 3, (dc, work Picot, 2 dc) in same sp, ★ ch 1, (2 dc, work Picot, 2 dc) in next ch-6 sp; repeat from ★ around, sc in first dc to form last ch-1 sp: 22 groups and 22 ch-1 sps.

Rnds 6-14: Repeat Rnds 4 and 5, 4 times; then repeat Rnd 4 once **more**; finish off: 22 ch-6 sps.

MIDDLE SECTION

Rnd 1: With **right** side facing, join Color B with dc in any ch-6 sp ***(see Joining With Dc, page 30)***; dc in same sp, ch 3, (3 dc in next ch-6 sp, ch 3) around, dc in same sp as first dc; join with slip st to first dc: 22 3-dc groups.

Rnd 2: Ch 1, (sc, work Picot, sc) in same st as joining, ★ ch 4, (sc, work Picot, sc) in center dc of next 3-dc group; repeat from ★ around, ch 1, dc in first sc to form last ch-4 sp: 22 ch-4 sps.

Rnd 3: Ch 3, dc in last ch-4 sp made, ch 3, (3 dc in next ch-4 sp, ch 3) around, dc in same sp as first dc; join with slip st to first dc: 22 3-dc groups and 22 ch-3 sps.

Rnds 4-12: Repeat Rnds 2 and 3, 4 times, then repeat Rnd 2 once **more**; finish off: 22 ch-4 sps.

TOP SECTION

Rnd 1: With **right** side facing, join Color C with sc in any ch-4 sp ***(see Joining With Sc, page 30)***; work Picot, sc in same sp, ★ ch 6, (sc, work Picot, sc) in next ch-4 sp; repeat from ★ around, ch 3, dc in first sc to form last ch-6 sp: 22 ch-6 sps.

Rnd 2: Ch 1, (sc, work Picot, sc) in last ch-6 sp made, ★ ch 6, (sc, work Picot, sc) in next ch-6 sp; repeat from ★ around, ch 3, dc in first sc to form last ch-6 sp.

Repeat Rnd 2 for pattern until piece measures approximately 17½" (44.5 cm) from beginning ch; do **not** finish off.

BAND

Rnd 1: Ch 3, dc in last ch-6 sp made, 5 dc in each ch-6 sp around, 3 dc in same sp as first dc; join with slip st to first dc: 110 dc.

Rnd 2: Ch 3, dc in next dc and in each dc around; join with slip st to first dc, finish off.

Rnd 3: With **right** side facing, join Color A with dc in any dc; dc in next dc and in each dc around; join with slip st to first dc.

Rnd 4: Ch 1, (slip st in next dc, ch 1) around; join with slip st to joining slip st, finish off.

STRAP

With Color A, ch 100.

Row 1 (Right side)**:** Hdc in third ch from hook **(2 skipped chs count as first hdc)** and in each ch across; finish off: 99 hdc.

Note: Mark Row 1 as **right** side.

Row 2: With **right** side facing and leaving a long end for sewing, join Color C with slip st in first hdc; ch 1 **(does not count as a st)**, hdc in each hdc across; do **not** cut yarn, finish off by pulling skein through last loop.

Row 3: With **right** side facing, join Color A with slip st in first hdc; ch 1, hdc in each hdc across; cut Color A, do **not** finish off.

Trim: Using Color C, ch 1, do **not** turn; (slip st, ch 1) evenly around; join with slip st to first st, finish off leaving a long end for sewing.

Sew ends of Strap to inside of Tote at each side.

Design by Cathy Hardy.

Air Plant Hanger

 EASY

Finished Size: 4" wide x 21" high (10 cm x 53.5 cm) (excluding hanger & loop fringe)

SHOPPING LIST

Yarn (Medium Weight) 

- ☐ Color A (Yellow) - 60 yards (55 meters)
- ☐ Color B (Variegated) - 40 yards (36.5 meters)

Crochet Hook

- ☐ Size 7 (4.5 mm) **or** size needed for gauge

Additional Supplies

- ☐ Yarn needle

GAUGE INFORMATION

7 dc and 3 rows = 2" (5 cm)

Gauge Swatch: 2" (5 cm) square

With Color A, ch 9.

Row 1: Dc in fourth ch from hook **(3 skipped chs count as first dc)** and in each ch across: 7 dc.

Rows 2-3: Ch 3 **(counts as first dc)**, turn; dc in next dc and in each dc across.

Finish off.

STITCH GUIDE

SHELL

(2 Dc, ch 1, 2 dc) in st or sp indicated.

DOUBLE CROCHET 3 TOGETHER

(abbreviated dc3tog) (uses next 3 dc)

★ YO, insert hook in **next** dc, YO and pull up a loop, YO and draw through 2 loops on hook; repeat from ★ 2 times **more**, YO and draw through all 4 loops on hook.

BOTTOM SECTION

Rnd 1 (Right side)**:** With Color A, make an adjustable loop to form a ring ***(Figs. 1a-d, page 30)***; ch 2, 5 dc in ring; join with slip st to top of beginning ch: 6 sts.

Note: Loop a short piece of yarn around any stitch to mark Rnd 1 as **right** side.

Rnd 2: Ch 3 **(counts as first dc, now and throughout)**, dc in same st, 2 dc in next dc and in each dc around; join with slip st to first dc: 12 dc.

Rnd 3: Ch 4 **(counts as first dc plus ch 1)**, dc in same st, skip next dc, ★ (dc, ch 1, dc) in next dc, skip next dc; repeat from ★ around; join with slip st to first dc: 12 dc and 6 ch-1 sps.

Rnd 4: Ch 3, 2 dc in next ch-1 sp, (dc in next 2 dc, 2 dc in next ch-1 sp) around to last dc, dc in last dc; join with slip st to first dc: 24 dc.

Rnd 5: Ch 1, (sc, ch 3, dc) in same st as joining, ★ skip next dc, (sc, ch 3, dc) in next dc; repeat from ★ 4 times **more**, skip next dc, sc in next dc, dc in next dc, skip next dc, work Shell in next dc, (ch 1, skip next 2 dc, work Shell in next dc) twice, skip next dc, dc in last dc; do **not** join.

Begin working in rows.

Row 1: Ch 3, **turn**; work Shell in next Shell (ch-1 sp), (ch 1, skip next ch-1 sp, work Shell in next Shell) twice, skip next 2 dc of same Shell, dc in next dc, leave remaining sts unworked: 3 Shells and 2 ch-1 sps.

Row 2: Ch 3, turn; work Shell in next Shell, ★ ch 3, working **around** next ch-1 *(Fig. 4, page 31)*, sc in ch-1 sp on row **below**, ch 3, work Shell in next Shell; repeat from ★ once **more**, dc in last dc.

Row 3: Ch 3, turn; work Shell in next Shell, ★ ch 1, skip next 2 ch-3 sps, work Shell in next Shell; repeat from ★ once **more**, dc in last dc: 3 Shells and 2 ch-1 sps.

Row 4: Ch 3, turn; work Shell in next Shell, ★ ch 1, skip next ch-1 sp, work Shell in next Shell; repeat from ★ once **more**, dc in last dc.

Row 5: Repeat Row 2.

Row 6: Ch 3, turn; 3 dc in next Shell, ★ skip next 2 ch-3 sps, 3 dc in next Shell; repeat from ★ once **more**, dc in last dc: 11 dc.

Rows 7-9: Ch 3, turn; dc in next dc and in each dc across.

Finish off leaving a long end for sewing.

MIDDLE SECTION

Using Color B, work same as Bottom Section.

Using photo as a guide for placement, sew top of Rnd 5 of Middle Section to top of last row of Bottom Section.

TOP SECTION

Using Color A, work same as Bottom Section through Row 6: 11 dc.

Row 7: Ch 3, turn; dc3tog, (ch 3, dc3tog) twice, dc in last dc; finish off.

Using photo as a guide for placement, sew top of Rnd 5 of Top Section to top of last row of Middle Section.

HANGER

With Color B, ch 16; join with slip st to form a ring, ch 6, with **right** side of Top Section facing, dc in first dc, ★ 2 dc in next ch-3 sp, ch 6, sc in ring, ch 6, 2 dc in same ch-3 sp; repeat from ★ once **more**, skip next st, dc in last dc, ch 6, 20 sc in ring, slip st in ring; finish off.

LOOP FRINGE

With Color B, make an adjustable ring; (ch 16, slip st in ring) 5 times; finish off leaving a long end for sewing.

Sew Loop Fringe to bottom of Bottom Section.

Place an air plant in each holder and give them an occasional misting.

Design by Cathy Hardy.

Bath Set

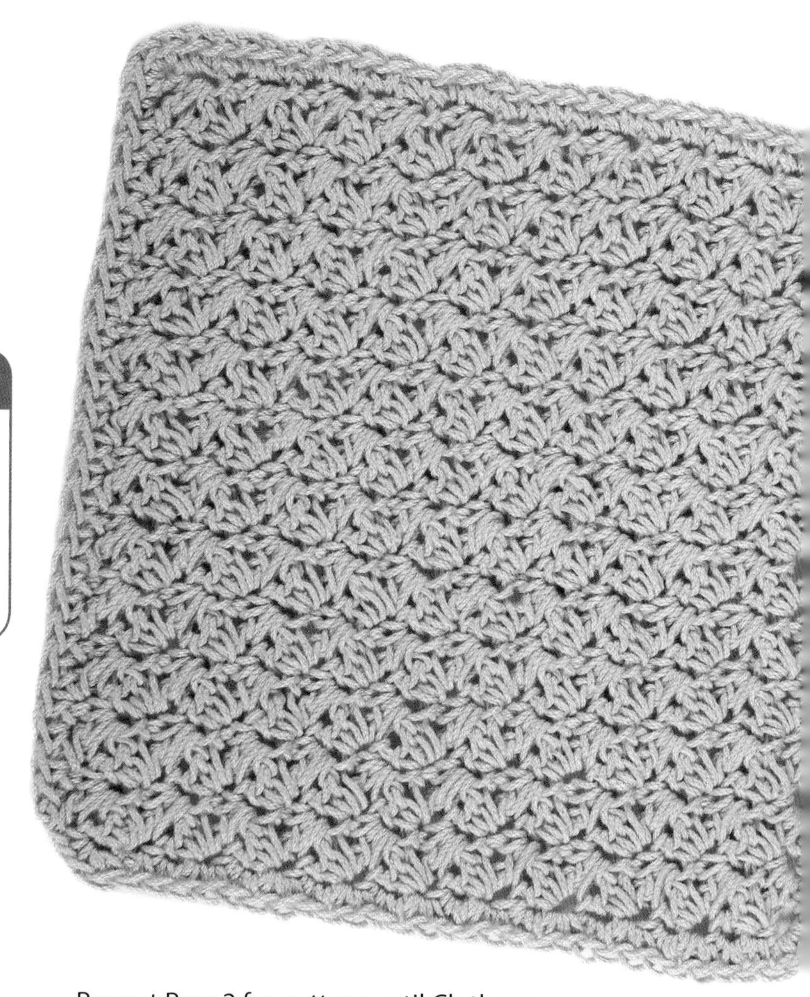

FACE CLOTH

 **EASY**

Finished Size: 8" (20.5 cm) square

SHOPPING LIST

Yarn (Medium Weight) 

☐ 75 yards (68.5 meters)

Crochet Hook

☐ Size J (6 mm) **or** size needed for gauge

GAUGE INFORMATION

In pattern, 10 sts = 3" (7.5 cm)

Gauge Swatch: 7½" (19 cm) wide

Work same as Cloth for 4 rows.

BODY

Ch 26.

Row 1: (Sc, dc) in second ch from hook, ★ skip next ch, (sc, dc) in next ch; repeat from ★ across to last 2 chs, skip next ch, sc in last ch: 25 sts.

Row 2: Ch 1, turn; (sc, dc) in first sc, ★ skip next dc, (sc, dc) in next sc; repeat from ★ across to last 2 sts, skip next dc, sc in last sc.

Repeat Row 2 for pattern until Cloth measures approximately 7½" (19 cm) from beginning ch.

EDGING

Ch 1, do **not** turn; sc in evenly around entire Cloth, working 3 sc in each corner ***(Fig. 2b, page 30)***; join with slip st to first sc, finish off.

FACE SCRUBBIE

EASY

Finished Size: 4" (10 cm) diameter

SHOPPING LIST

Yarn (Medium Weight) MEDIUM 4

☐ Main Color - 15 yards (13.5 meters) **each**

☐ Contrasting Color - 10 yards (9 meters) **each**

Crochet Hook

☐ Size G (4 mm) **or** size needed for gauge

GAUGE INFORMATION

Gauge Swatch: 2½" (6.25 cm) diameter

Work same as Scrubbie through Rnd 2 of Base.

BASE

Rnd 1 (Right side)**:** With Main Color, make an adjustable loop to form a ring ***(Figs. 1a-d, page 30)***; (sc, hdc, 12 dc) in ring; do **not** join, place marker to indicate beginning of rnd ***(see Markers, page 30)***: 14 sts.

Note: Loop a short piece of yarn around any stitch to mark Rnd 1 as **right** side.

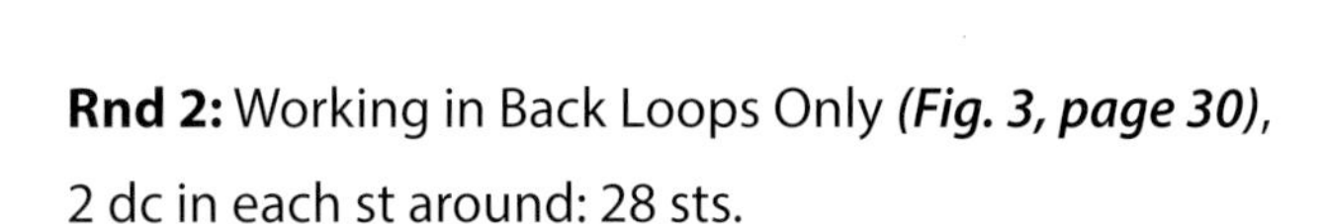

Rnd 2: Working in Back Loops Only ***(Fig. 3, page 30)***, 2 dc in each st around: 28 sts.

Rnd 3: Working in Back Loops Only, (dc in next dc, 2 dc in next dc) around to marker; remove marker, hdc in next dc, sc in next dc, slip st in next dc; finish off: 42 sts.

TRIM

With **right** side facing and working in free loops of Base ***(Fig. 2a, page 30)***, join Contrasting Color with slip st in first sc on Rnd 1; (ch 3, slip st) in each st around Base to slip st at end of Rnd 3; (ch 1, slip st) in both loops of each dc around; finish off.

BATH POUF

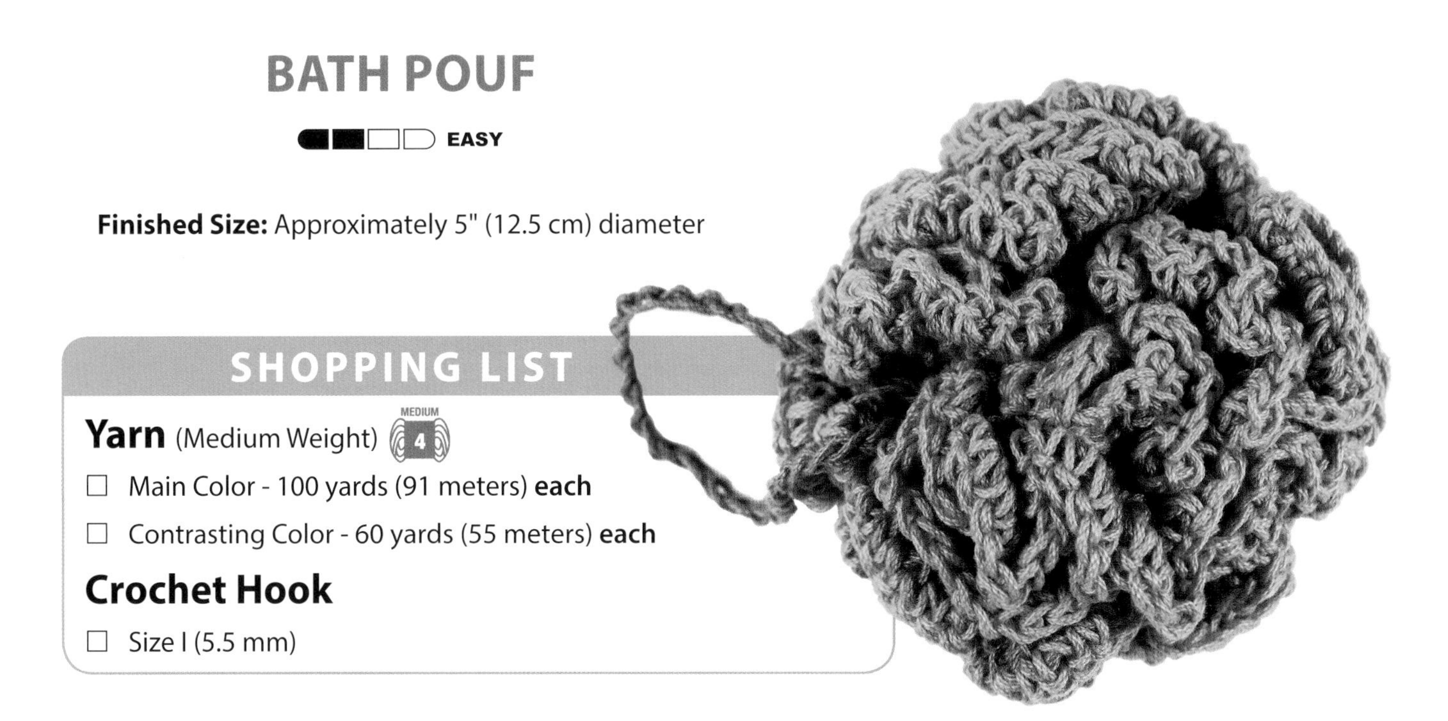

EASY

Finished Size: Approximately 5" (12.5 cm) diameter

SHOPPING LIST

Yarn (Medium Weight) MEDIUM 4

- ☐ Main Color - 100 yards (91 meters) **each**
- ☐ Contrasting Color - 60 yards (55 meters) **each**

Crochet Hook

- ☐ Size I (5.5 mm)

Gauge is not important. Your Pouf can be slightly smaller or larger without changing the overall effect.

BASE

Rnd 1: With Main Color, make an adjustable ring ***(Figs. 1a-d, page 30)***; ch 40 for hanger, being careful **not** to twist ch, slip st in ring, ch 5 **(counts as first dc plus ch 2)**, (dc, ch 2) 14 times in ring; working in **front** of hanger, join with slip st to first dc: 15 ch-2 sps.

Rnds 2 and 3: Slip st in first ch-2 sp, ch 5, (dc, ch 2) 4 times in same sp, (dc, ch 2) 5 times in each ch-2 sp around; join with slip st to first dc.

Finish off.

TRIM

With same side facing, join Contrasting Color with sc in any ch-2 sp ***(see Joining With Sc, page 30)***; sc in next dc, (sc in next ch-2 sp, sc in next dc) around; join with slip st to first sc, finish off.

Coaster Set

 EASY

Finished Sizes:

Coaster - 4¾" (12 cm)

Container - 6" diameter

x 2" deep (15 cm x 5 cm)

SHOPPING LIST

Yarn (Medium Weight) 

Note: Yarn amounts will make 6 coasters and 1 container.

[2 ounces, 95 yards (56.7 grams, 86 meters) per skein**]**:

- ☐ Color A (Variegated) - 2 skeins
- ☐ Color B (Yellow) - 30 yards (27.5 meters)
- ☐ Color C (Green) - 30 yards (27.5 meters)
- ☐ Color D (Pink) - 30 yards (27.5 meters)

Crochet Hook

- ☐ Size H (5 mm) **or** size needed for gauge

GAUGE INFORMATION

Gauge Swatch #1:

2¾" (7 cm) diameter

Work same as Coaster through Rnd 2.

Gauge Swatch #2:

2¼" (5.75 cm) diameter

Work same as Container through Rnd 2, page 20.

STITCH GUIDE

2-DC CLUSTER (uses one sp)

★ YO, insert hook in sp indicated, YO and pull up a loop, YO and draw through 2 loops on hook; repeat from ★ once **more**, YO and draw through all 3 loops on hook.

3-DC CLUSTER (uses one sp)

★ YO, insert hook in sp indicated, YO and pull up a loop, YO and draw through 2 loops on hook; repeat from ★ 2 times **more**, YO and draw through all 4 loops on hook.

COASTER

(Make 6 working Rnds 2-4 in desired colors)

With Color A, ch 5; join with slip st to form a ring.

Rnd 1 (Right side)**:** Ch 3 **(counts as first dc)**, 10 dc in ring; join with slip st to first dc, finish off: 11 dc.

Note: Loop a short piece of yarn around any stitch to mark Rnd 1 as **right** side.

Rnd 2: With **right** side facing, join next color with slip st in sp **between** any 2 dc ***(Fig. 5, page 31)***; ch 2, work 2-dc Cluster in same sp, ch 2, skip next dc, ★ work 3-dc Cluster in sp **before** next dc, ch 2, skip next dc; repeat from ★ around; join with slip st to top of first 2-dc Cluster, finish off: 11 ch-2 sps.

Rnd 3: With **right** side facing, join next color with sc in any ch-2 sp ***(see Joining With Sc, page 30)***; ch 3, (sc in next ch-2 sp, ch 3) around; join with slip st to first sc, finish off.

Rnd 4: With **right** side facing, join next color with slip st in any ch-3 sp; ch 2, (dc, ch 4, work 2-dc Cluster) in same sp, work (2-dc Cluster, ch 4, 2-dc Cluster) in each ch-3 sp around; join with slip st to first dc, finish off.

Rnd 5: With **right** side facing, join Color A with sc in any ch-4 sp; 4 sc in same sp, skip next 2-dc Cluster, sc in sp **before** next 2-dc Cluster, ★ 5 sc in next ch-4 sp, skip next 2-dc Cluster, sc in sp **before** next 2-dc Cluster; repeat from ★ around; join with slip st to first sc, finish off.

CONTAINER

BOTTOM

Rnd 1 (Right side)**:** With Color A, ch 4, 11 dc in fourth ch from hook; join with slip st to top of beginning ch: 12 sts.

Note: Loop a short piece of yarn around any stitch to mark Rnd 1 as **right** side.

Rnd 2: Ch 3 **(counts as first dc, now and throughout)**, dc in same st, 2 dc in next dc and in each dc around; join with slip st to first dc: 24 dc.

Rnd 3: Ch 3, dc in same st as joining and in next dc, (2 dc in next dc, dc in next dc) around; join with slip st to first dc: 36 dc.

Rnd 4: Ch 3, dc in same st as joining and in next 2 dc, (2 dc in next dc, dc in next 2 dc) around; join with slip st to first dc: 48 dc.

Rnd 5: Ch 3, dc in same st as joining and in next 3 dc, (2 dc in next dc, dc in next 3 dc) around; join with slip st to first dc: 60 dc.

Rnd 6: Ch 1, working in Back Loops Only ***(Fig. 3, page 30)***, 2 sc in same st as joining, sc in next 4 dc, (2 sc in next dc, sc in next 4 dc) around; join with slip st to Front Loop Only of first sc, do **not** finish off: 72 sc.

OUTER SIDES

Rnd 1: Ch 1, **turn**; sc in Back Loop Only of each sc around; join with slip st to **both** loops of first sc.

Rnd 2: Ch 1, do **not** turn; working in both loops, sc in same st as joining, ch 1, skip next sc, ★ sc in next sc, ch 1, skip next sc; repeat from ★ around; join with slip st to first sc: 36 sc and 36 ch-1 sps.

Rnd 3: Ch 1, sc in same st as joining, working **behind** next ch-1 ***(Fig. 4, page 31)***, dc in st one row **below** ch-1, sc in next sc, working in **front** of next ch-1, dc in st one row **below** ch-1, ★ sc in next sc, working **behind** next ch-1, dc in st one row **below** ch-1, sc in next sc, working in **front** of next ch-1, dc in st one row **below** ch-1; repeat from ★ around; join with slip st to first sc: 72 sts.

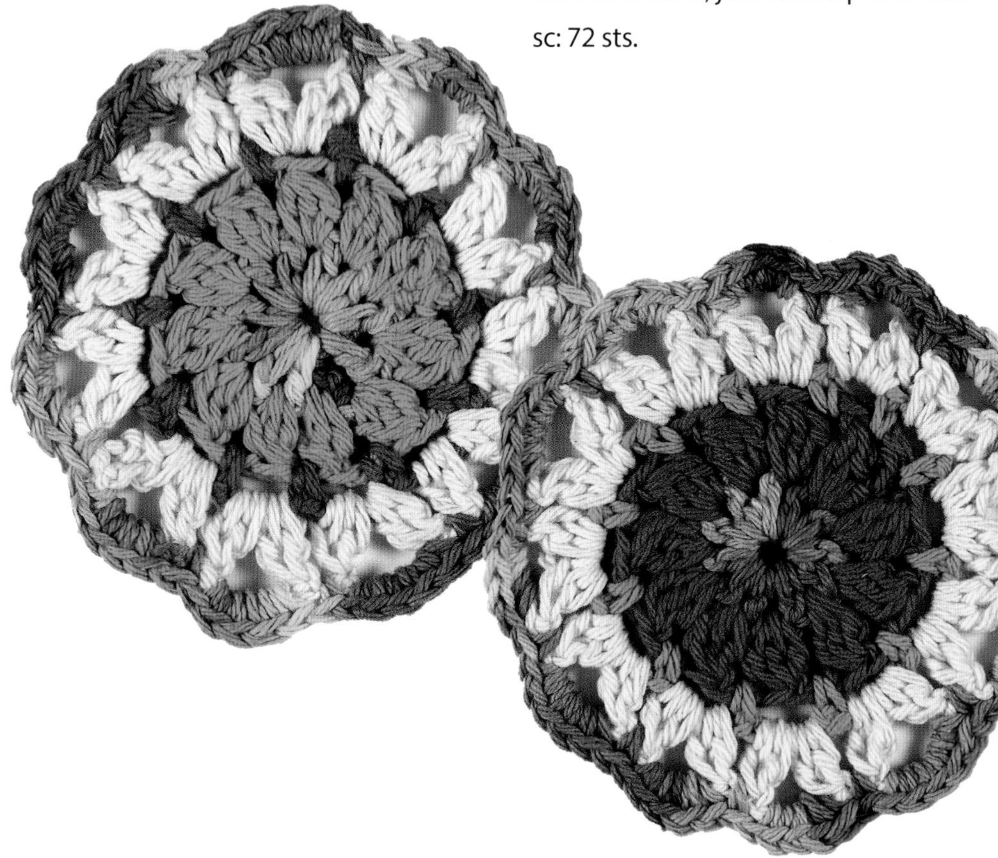

Rnd 4: Ch 1, sc in same st as joining, ch 1, skip next dc, ★ sc in next sc, ch 1, skip next dc; repeat from ★ around; join with slip st to first sc: 36 sc and 36 ch-1 sps.

Rnd 5: Ch 1, sc in same st as joining, working in **front** of next ch-1, dc in dc one row **below** ch-1, sc in next sc, working **behind** next ch-1, dc in dc one row **below** ch-1, ★ sc in next sc, working in **front** of next ch-1, dc in dc one row **below** ch-1, sc in next sc, working **behind** next ch-1, dc in dc one row **below** ch-1; repeat from ★ around; join with slip st to first sc: 72 sts.

Rnd 6: Repeat Rnd 4.

Rnd 7: Repeat Rnd 3; finish off.

INNER SIDES

Rnd 1: With **right** side of Bottom facing and working in free loops on Rnd 5 ***(Fig. 2b, page 30)***, join yarn with sc in any dc ***(see Joining With Sc, page 30)***; sc in each dc around; join with slip st to first sc: 60 sc.

Rnd 2: Ch 1, sc in same st as joining, ch 1, skip next sc, ★ sc in next sc, ch 1, skip next sc; repeat from ★ around; join with slip st to first sc: 30 sc and 30 ch-1 sps.

Rnds 3-7: Work same as Outer Sides; do **not** finish off.

JOINING

To decrease, insert hook in next st on **both** pieces, YO and pull up a loop, insert hook in **next** st on Outer Sides **and** in **same** st on Inner Sides, YO and pull up a loop, YO and draw through all 3 loops on hook.

Ch 1, turn; with Outer Sides facing and working in **both** loops of **both** pieces, sc in first 3 sts, decrease, (sc in next 4 sts, decrease) around; join with slip st to first sc, finish off.

Designs by Patty Kowaleski.

Dishcloth & Towel

 EASY

Finished Sizes:

Dishcloth - 9½" (24 cm) square

Dishtowel - 15¼" wide x 18½" high (38.5 cm x 47 cm)

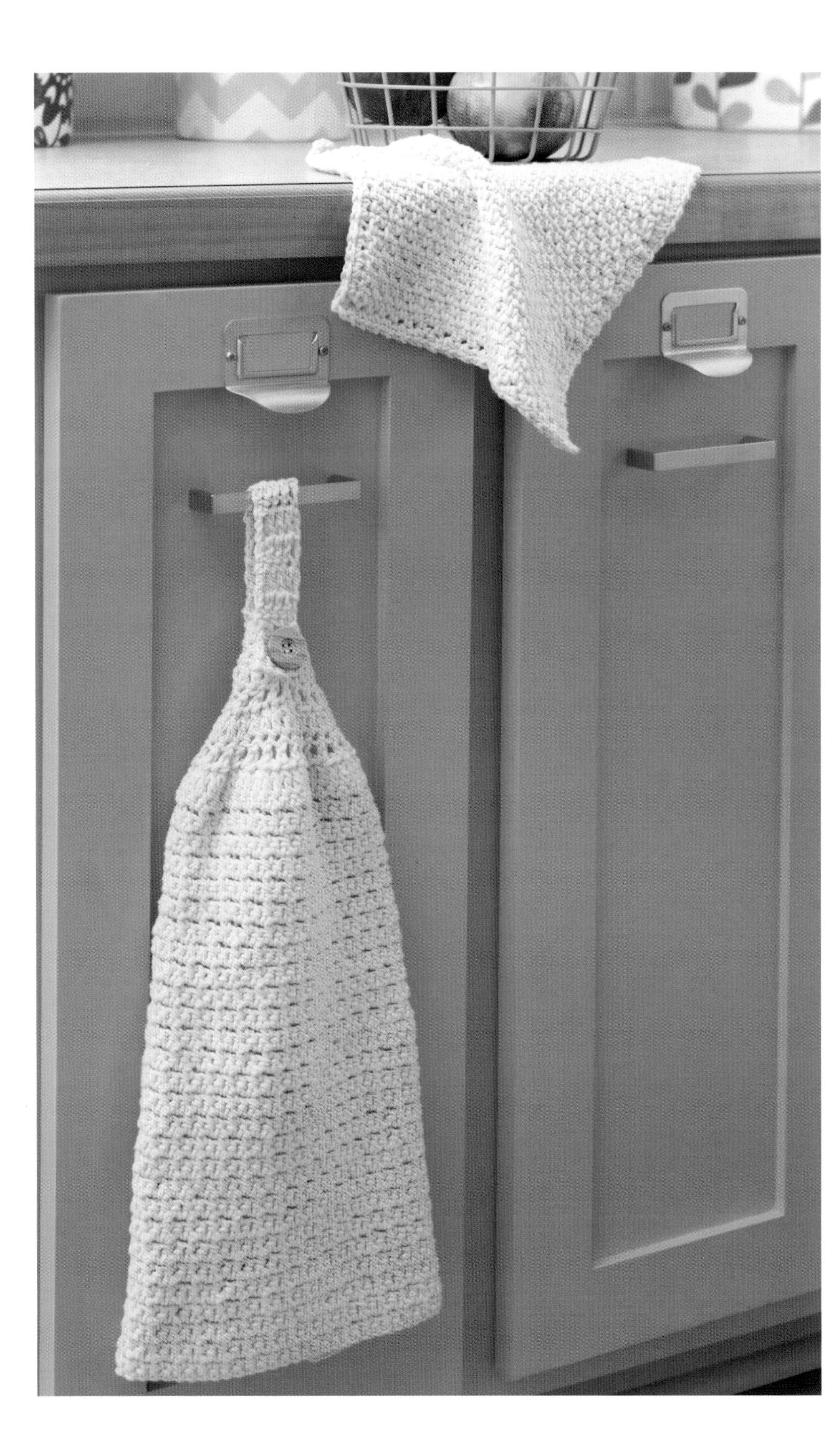

SHOPPING LIST

Yarn (Medium Weight) 

[2.5 ounces, 120 yards (70.9 grams, 109 meters) per skein]:

- ☐ 3 skeins

Crochet Hook

- ☐ Size H (5 mm) **or** size needed for gauge

Additional Supplies

(For Dishtowel only)

- ☐ Button
- ☐ Sewing needle and thread

GAUGE INFORMATION

In pattern,

8 sps and 12 rows = 3¾" (9.5 cm)

Gauge Swatch: 3¾" (9.5 cm) square

Ch 18.

Rows 1-12: Work same as Dishcloth: 8 sps.

Finish off.

DISHCLOTH

Ch 42.

Row 1: Sc in fourth ch from hook, ★ ch 1, skip next ch, sc in next ch; repeat from ★ across: 20 sps.

Row 2: Ch 3, turn; sc in first ch-1 sp, (ch 1, sc in next sp) across.

Repeat Row 2 for pattern until piece measures 9" (23 cm) from beginning ch, working an even number of rows.

Edging: Ch 1, turn; (sc, ch 3, sc) in first ch-1 sp, ch 1, (sc in next ch-1 sp, ch 1) across to last ch-3 sp, (sc, ch 3, sc) in last ch-3 sp, ch 1; working in end of rows, skip first 2 rows, † sc in next row, ch 1, skip next row †, repeat from † to † across; working in sps across beginning ch, (sc, ch 3, sc) in first sp, ch 1, (sc in next sp, ch 1) across to last sp, (sc, ch 3, sc) in last sp, ch 1; working in end of rows, skip first 2 rows, repeat from † to † across; join with slip st to first sc, finish off.

DISHTOWEL

BODY

Ch 66.

Row 1 (Right side)**:** Sc in second ch from hook and in each ch across: 65 sc.

Note: Loop a short piece of yarn around any stitch to mark Row 1 as **right** side.

Row 2: Ch 1, turn; sc in first sc, ★ ch 1, skip next sc, sc in next sc; repeat from ★ across: 33 sc and 32 ch-1 sps.

Row 3: Ch 1, turn; sc in each sc and in each ch-1 sp across: 65 sc.

Repeat Rows 2 and 3 for pattern until piece measures approximately 13" (33 cm) from beginning ch, ending by working Row 3.

SHAPING

Row 1: Ch 3 **(counts as first dc, now and throughout)**, turn; dc in next sc and in each sc across.

Row 2: Ch 3, turn; (skip next dc, dc in next dc) across: 33 dc.

Row 3: Ch 3, turn; dc in next dc and in each dc across.

Rows 4-8: Repeat Rows 2 and 3 twice, then repeat Row 2 once **more**: 5 dc.

Rows 9-17: Ch 3, turn; dc in next dc and in each dc across.

Row 18: Ch 3, turn; dc in next dc, ch 1, skip next dc **(buttonhole made)**, dc in last 2 dc: 4 dc and one ch-1 sp.

Row 19: Ch 3, turn; dc in next dc and in next ch-1 sp, dc in last 2 dc; finish off.

With **right** side facing, sew button to center dc on Row 5 of Shaping.

Designs by Roberta Maier.

Potholder

EASY

Finished Size: 6½" (16.5 cm) square

SHOPPING LIST

Yarn (Medium Weight) MEDIUM 4

[2 ounces, 95 yards

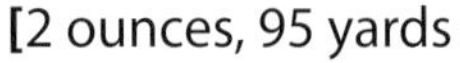

(56.7 grams, 86 meters) per skein]:

☐ 1 skein

Crochet Hook

☐ Size 7 (4.5 mm)
or size needed for gauge

Additional Supplies

☐ Yarn needle

GAUGE INFORMATION

In pattern, 10 sts = 2" (5 cm)

Gauge Swatch: 9" (22.75 cm) long

Work same as Potholder for 4 rnds.

STITCH GUIDE

SINGLE CROCHET 2 TOGETHER
(abbreviated sc2tog)

Pull up a loop in each of next 2 sts, YO and draw through all 3 loops on hook.

BODY

Ch 43.

Rnd 1 (Right side)**:** 3 Sc in second ch from hook, (sc2tog, ch 1) across to last ch, 3 sc in last ch; working in free loops of beginning ch ***(Fig. 2b, page 30)***, (sc2tog, ch 1) 20 times; do **not** join: 86 sts.

Pattern: Working in Back Loops Only ***(Fig. 3, page 30)***, (sc2tog, ch 1) around until piece measures approximately 4½" (11.5 cm) from beginning ch **or** until sides equal one half of width, ending at center of one side.

HANGER

(Sc, ch 12, sc) in next st; finish off leaving a long end for sewing.

With the Potholder flat, bring the stitches at both folds together and flatten piece to form a square with the opening placed diagonally ***(Figs. A & B)***; whipstitch closed ***(Fig. 8, page 31)***.

Fig. A

Fig. B

Placemat Set

EASY

Finished Sizes:

Placemat - 14½" x 20" (37 cm x 51 cm)

Coaster - 4" (10 cm) diameter

Napkin Ring - 3¼" long x 6" circumference (8.5 cm x 15 cm)

SHOPPING LIST

Yarn (Medium Weight) 

[3.5 ounces, 186 yards (100 grams, 170 meters) per skein]:

- ☐ Main Color (Brown) - 2 skeins
- ☐ Color A (Yellow) - 66 yards (60.5 meters)
- ☐ Color B (Green) - 66 yards (60.5 meters)

Crochet Hook

- ☐ Size E (3.5 mm) **or** size needed for gauge

Additional Supplies

- ☐ Yarn needle

GAUGE INFORMATION

16 dc and 8 rows = 4" (10 cm)

Gauge Swatch: 4" (10 cm) square

With Main Color, ch 18.

Row 1: Dc in fourth ch from hook **(3 skipped chs count as first dc)** and in each ch across: 16 dc.

Rows 2-8: Ch 3 **(counts as first dc)**, turn; dc in next dc and in each dc across.

Finish off.

PLACEMAT

STRIPES - FIRST END

With Main Color, ch 59.

Row 1 (Right side)**:** Dc in fourth ch from hook **(3 skipped chs count as first dc)** and in each ch across: 57 dc.

Note: Loop a short piece of yarn around any stitch to mark Row 1 as **right** side.

Row 2: Ch 3 **(counts as first dc, now and throughout)**, turn; dc in next 2 dc, (ch 3, skip next 3 dc, dc in next 3 dc) across; finish off: 30 dc and 9 ch-3 sps.

Row 3: With **right** side facing, join Color A with sc in first dc ***(see Joining With Sc, page 30)***; sc in next 2 dc, ★ working in **front** of next ch-3 ***(Fig. 4, page 31)***, dc in next 3 dc on row **below**, sc in next 3 dc on previous row; repeat from ★ across: 57 sts.

Row 4: Ch 3, turn; dc in next 2 sc, (ch 3, skip next 3 dc, dc in next 3 sc) across; finish off: 30 dc and 9 ch-3 sps.

Rows 5 and 6: With Color B, repeat Rows 3 and 4.

Row 7: With Main Color, repeat Row 3; do **not** finish off.

BODY

Row 1: Ch 3, turn; dc in next sc and in each st across.

Repeat Row 1 until Placemat measures approximately 17½" (44.5 cm) from beginning ch, ending by working a **right** side row; do **not** finish off.

STRIPES - SECOND END

Row 1: Repeat Row 2 of First End.

Rows 2 and 3: With Color B, repeat Rows 3 and 4.

Rows 4 and 5: Repeat Rows 3 and 4.

Row 6: With Main Color, repeat Row 3.

Row 7: Ch 3, turn; dc in next sc and in each st across; finish off.

EDGING

Rnd 1: With **right** side facing, join Color A with sc in any st; sc evenly around entire piece, working 3 sc in each corner ***(Fig. 2b, page 30)***; join with slip st to first sc, finish off.

Rnd 2: With **right** side facing, join Color B with slip st in any sc; working from **left** to **right**, work reverse sc in each sc around ***(Figs. 6a-d, page 31)***; join with slip st to first st, finish off.

NAPKIN RING

With Main Color, ch 24; being careful **not** to twist ch, join with slip st to form a ring.

Rnd 1 (Right side)**:** Ch 3 **(counts as first dc, now and throughout)**, dc in next ch and in each ch around; join with slip st to first dc: 24 dc.

Note: Loop a short piece of yarn around any stitch to mark Rnd 1 as **right** side.

Rnd 2: Ch 3, dc in next 2 dc, ch 3, skip next 3 dc, (dc in next 3 dc, ch 3, skip next 3 dc) around; join with slip st to first dc, finish off: 12 dc and 4 ch-3 sps.

Rnd 3: With **right** side facing, join Color A with sc in same st as joining ***(see Joining With Sc, page 30)***; sc in next 2 dc, working in **front** of next ch-3 ***(Fig. 4, page 31)***, dc in next 3 dc on rnd **below**, ★ sc in next 3 dc on previous rnd, working in **front** of next ch-3, dc in next 3 dc on rnd **below**; repeat from ★ around; join with slip st to first sc: 24 sts.

Rnd 4: Ch 3, dc in next 2 sc, ch 3, skip next 3 dc, (dc in next 3 sc, ch 3, skip next 3 dc) around; join with slip st to first dc, finish off: 12 dc and 4 ch-3 sps.

Rnds 5 and 6: With Color B, repeat Rnds 3 and 4.

Rnd 7: With Main Color, repeat Rnd 3.

Rnd 8: Ch 3, dc in next sc and in each st around; join with slip st to first dc, finish off.

Edging - First Side: With **right** side facing, join Color A with sc in same st as joining; working from **left** to **right**, work reverse sc in each dc around ***(Figs. 6a-d, page 31)***; join with slip st to first st, finish off.

Edging - Second Side: With **right** side facing and working in free loops of beginning ch ***(Fig. 2b, page 30)***, join Color B with slip st in any ch; ch 1, working from **left** to **right**, work reverse sc in each ch around; join with slip st to first st, finish off.

COASTER

Rnd 1 (Right side)**:** With Main Color, make an adjustable loop to form a ring ***(Figs. 1a-d, page 30)***; ch 2, 11 dc in ring; join with slip st to top of beginning ch, finish off: 12 sts.

Note: Loop a short piece of yarn around any stitch to mark Rnd 1 as **right** side.

Rnd 2: With **right** side facing, join Color A with dc in same st as joining ***(see Joining With Dc, page 30)***; 2 dc in same st, ch 2, skip next dc, (3 dc in next dc, ch 2, skip next dc) around; join with slip st to first dc, finish off: 18 dc and 6 ch-2 sps.

Rnd 3: With **right** side facing, join Color B with sc in same st as joining ***(see Joining With Sc, page 30)***; sc in next 2 dc, working in **front** of next ch-2 ***(Fig. 4, page 31)***, 3 dc in next dc on rnd **below**, ★ sc in next 3 dc on previous rnd, working in **front** of next ch-2, 3 dc in next dc on rnd **below**; repeat from ★ around; join with slip st to first sc, finish off: 36 sts.

Rnd 4: With **right** side facing, join Main Color with dc in same st as joining; dc in same st and in next 2 sc, (2 dc in next st, dc in next 2 sts) around; join with slip st to first dc, finish off: 48 dc.

Rnd 5: With **right** side facing, join either Color A or Color B with slip st in same st as joining; ch 1, work reverse sc in each dc around ***(Figs. 6a-d, page 31)***; join with slip st to first st, finish off.

Designs by Cathy Hardy.

Half Hexagon Rug

 EASY

Finished Size:

17" x 40" (43 cm x 101.5 cm)

SHOPPING LIST

Yarn

(Medium Weight) 

[2.5 ounces, 120 yards

(70.9 grams, 109 meters) per ball]:

- ☐ Color A (Grey) - 3 balls
- ☐ Color B (Yellow) - 2 balls
- ☐ Color C (Ecru) - 2 balls

Crochet Hook

- ☐ Size J (6 mm)

  or size needed for gauge

GAUGE INFORMATION

3 Puff Sts = 2" (5 cm)

Gauge Swatch: 6" (15 cm) wide

Work same as Rug through Row 4.

STITCH GUIDE

PUFF ST (uses one sp)

★ YO, insert hook in sp indicated, YO and pull up a loop; repeat from ★ 3 times **more**, YO and draw through all 9 loops on hook, ch 1 to close.

RUG

With Color B, ch 5; join with slip st to form a ring.

Row 1: Work 5 Puff Sts in ring; do **not** join.

Row 2 (Right side)**:** Turn; work 2 Puff Sts in each sp (between Puff Sts) across ***(Fig. 5, page 31)***: 8 Puff Sts.

Row 3: Turn; work 2 Puff Sts in first sp, (work Puff St in next sp, work 2 Puff Sts in next sp) 3 times: 11 Puff Sts.

Row 4: Turn; work 2 Puff Sts in first sp, work Puff St in next 2 sps, ★ work 2 Puff Sts in next sp **(corner made)**, work Puff St in next 2 sps; repeat from ★ once **more**, work 2 Puff Sts in last sp: 14 Puff Sts.

Row 5: Turn; work 2 Puff Sts in first sp, ★ work Puff St in each sp across to corner sp, work 2 Puff Sts in corner sp; repeat from ★ once **more**, work Puff St in each sp across to last sp, work 2 Puff Sts in last sp: 17 Puff Sts.

Rows 6-30: Repeat Row 5 working in the following stripe sequence: 1 Row Color B, 2 rows Color C, 6 rows Color A, 2 rows Color C, 6 rows Color B, 2 rows Color C, 6 rows Color A: 92 Puff Sts.

Edging: Working from **left** to **right**, ch 2, work reverse hdc in first Puff St ***(Figs. 7a-d, page 31)***, (ch 1, work reverse hdc in next Puff St) across, slip st in last st; finish off.

Design by Carole Rutter Tippett.

General Instructions

ABBREVIATIONS

ch(s)	chain(s)
cm	centimeters
dc	double crochet(s)
dc3tog	double crochet 3 together
hdc	half double crochet(s)
LSC	Long single crochet
mm	millimeters
Rnd(s)	Round(s)
sc	single crochet(s)
sc2tog	single crochet 2 together
sp(s)	space(s)
st(s)	stitch(es)
YO	yarn over

SYMBOLS & TERMS

★ — work instructions following ★ as many **more** times as indicated in addition to the first time.

† to † — work all instructions from first † to second † **as many** times as specified.

( ) or [ ] — work enclosed instructions **as many** times as specified by the number immediately following **or** work all enclosed instructions in the stitch or space indicated **or** contains explanatory remarks.

colon (:) — the number(s) given after a colon at the end of a row or round denote(s) the number of stitches or spaces you should have on that row or round.

GAUGE

Exact gauge is **essential** for proper size. Before beginning your project, make a sample swatch in the yarn and hook specified in the individual instructions. After completing the swatch, measure it, counting your stitches and rows carefully. If your swatch is larger or smaller than specified, **make another, changing hook size to get the correct gauge**. Keep trying until you find the size hook that will give you the specified gauge.

CROCHET TERMINOLOGY		
UNITED STATES		INTERNATIONAL
slip stitch (slip st)	=	single crochet (sc)
single crochet (sc)	=	double crochet (dc)
half double crochet (hdc)	=	half treble crochet (htr)
double crochet (dc)	=	treble crochet (tr)
treble crochet (tr)	=	double treble crochet (dtr)
double treble crochet (dtr)	=	triple treble crochet (ttr)
triple treble crochet (tr tr)	=	quadruple treble crochet (qtr)
skip	=	miss

Yarn Weight Symbol & Names	LACE 0	SUPER FINE 1	FINE 2	LIGHT 3	MEDIUM 4	BULKY 5	SUPER BULKY 6	JUMBO 7
Type of Yarns in Category	Fingering, size 10 crochet thread	Sock, Fingering, Baby	Sport, Baby	DK, Light Worsted	Worsted, Afghan, Aran	Chunky, Craft, Rug	Super Bulky, Roving	Jumbo, Roving
Crochet Gauge* Ranges in Single Crochet to 4" (10 cm)	32-42 sts**	21-32 sts	16-20 sts	12-17 sts	11-14 sts	8-11 sts	6-9 sts	5 sts and fewer
Advised Hook Size Range	Steel*** 6 to 8, Regular hook B-1	B-1 to E-4	E-4 to 7	7 to I-9	I-9 to K-10½	K-10½ to M/N-13	M/N-13 to Q	Q and larger

*GUIDELINES ONLY: The chart above reflects the most commonly used gauges and hook sizes for specific yarn categories.

** Lace weight yarns are usually crocheted with larger hooks to create lacy openwork patterns. Accordingly, a gauge range is difficult to determine. Always follow the gauge stated in your pattern.

*** Steel crochet hooks are sized differently from regular hooks–the higher the number, the smaller the hook, which is the reverse of regular hook sizing.

CROCHET HOOKS

U.S.	B-1	C-2	D-3	E-4	F-5	G-6	7	H-8	I-9	J-10	K-10½	L-11	M/N-13	N/P-15	P/Q	Q	S
Metric - mm	2.25	2.75	3.25	3.5	3.75	4	4.5	5	5.5	6	6.5	8	9	10	15	16	19

BEGINNER	Projects for first-time crocheters using basic stitches. Minimal shaping.
EASY	Projects using yarn with basic stitches, repetitive stitch patterns, simple color changes, and simple shaping and finishing.
INTERMEDIATE	Projects using a variety of techniques, such as basic lace patterns or color patterns, mid-level shaping and finishing.
EXPERIENCED	Projects with intricate stitch patterns, techniques and dimension, such as non-repeating patterns, multi-color techniques, fine threads, small hooks, detailed shaping and refined finishing.

MARKERS

Markers are used to help distinguish the beginning of each round being worked. Use a purchased marker or place a 2" (5 cm) scrap piece of yarn before the first stitch of each round, moving the marker after each round is complete.

JOINING WITH SC

When instructed to join with sc, begin with a slip knot on hook. Insert hook in stitch indicated, YO and pull up a loop, YO and draw through both loops on hook.

JOINING WITH DC

When instructed to join with dc, begin with a slip knot on hook. YO, holding loop on hook, insert hook in stitch indicated, YO and pull up a loop (3 loops on hook), (YO and draw through 2 loops on hook) twice.

ADJUSTABLE LOOP

Wind yarn around two fingers to form a ring ***(Fig. 1a)***. Slide yarn off fingers and grasp the strands at the top of the ring ***(Fig. 1b)***. Insert hook from **front** to **back** into the ring, pull up a loop, YO and draw through loop on hook to lock ring ***(Fig. 1c)*** (st made does **not** count as part of beginning ch of first rnd). Working around both strands, follow instructions to work sts in the ring, then pull yarn tail to close ***(Fig. 1d)***.

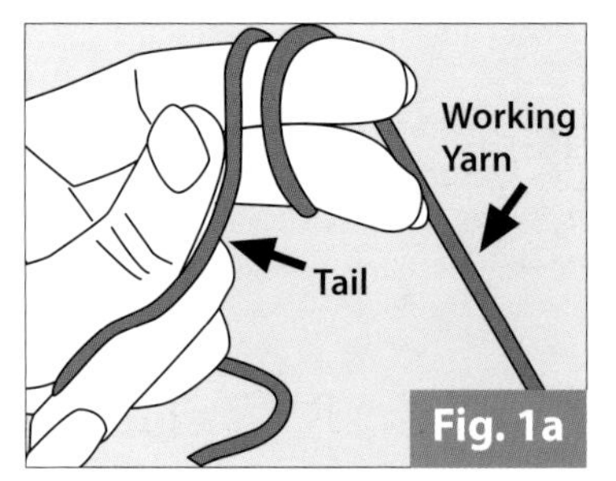

Fig. 1a

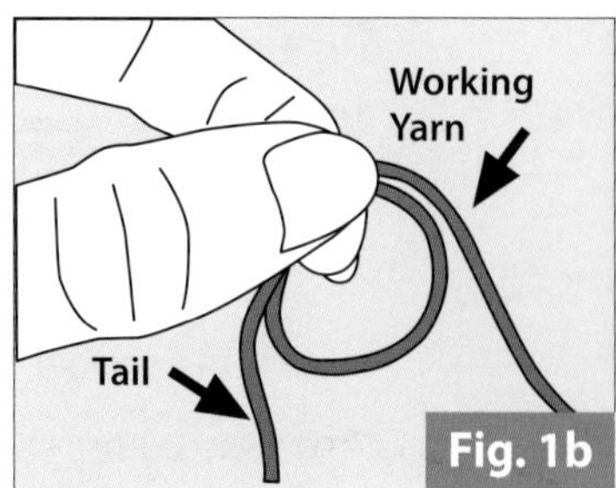

Fig. 1b

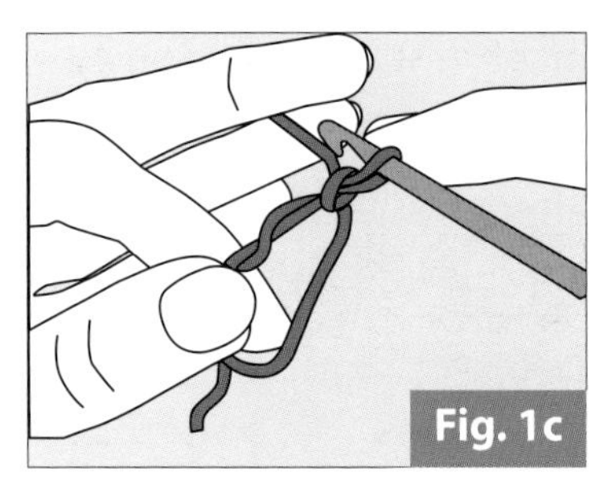
Fig. 1c

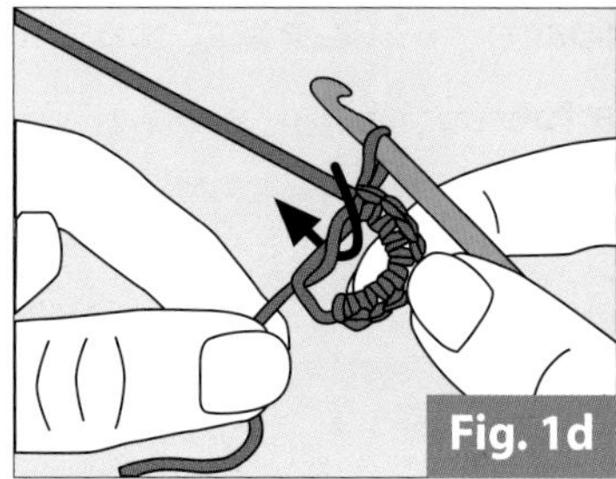
Fig. 1d

FREE LOOPS OF A CHAIN

After working in Back or Front Loops Only on a row or round, there will be a ridge of unused loops. These are called the free loops. Later, when instructed to work in the free loops of the same row or round, work in these loops ***(Fig. 2a)***. When instructed to work in free loops of a chain, work in loop indicated by arrow ***(Fig. 2b)***.

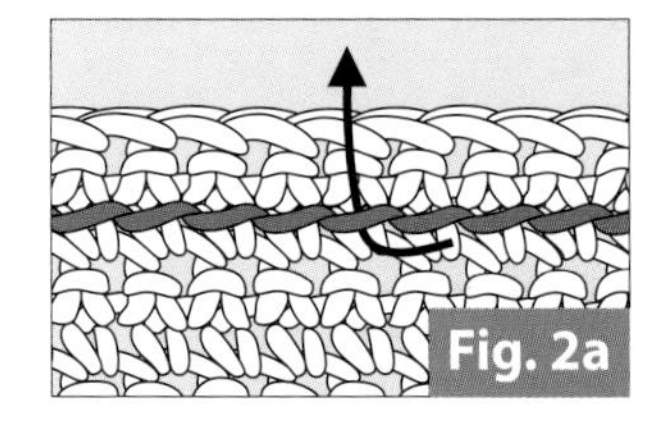
Fig. 2a

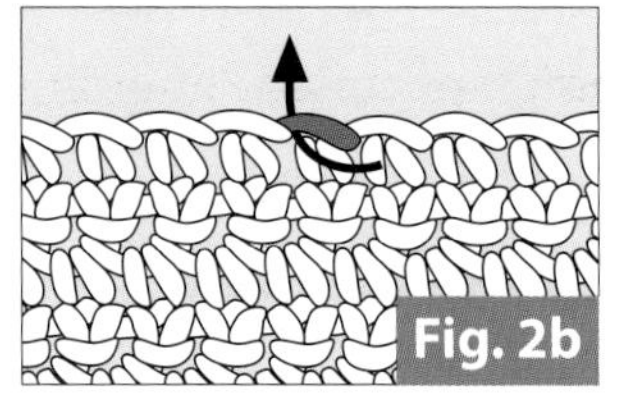
Fig. 2b

BACK OR FRONT LOOPS ONLY

Work only in loop(s) indicated by arrow ***(Fig. 3)***.

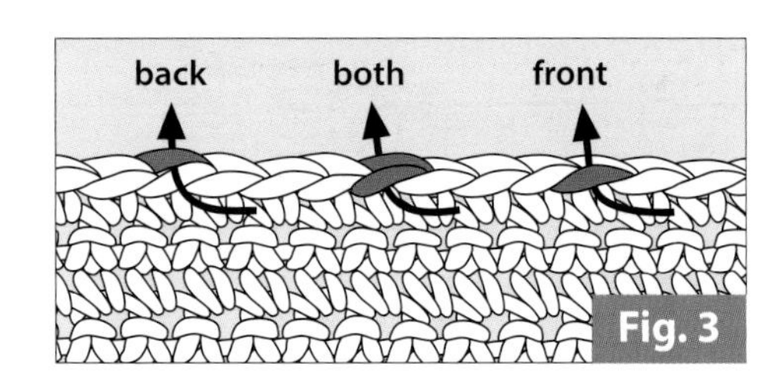

Fig. 3

WORKING IN FRONT OF, AROUND, OR BEHIND A STITCH

Work in stitch or space indicated, inserting hook in direction of arrow ***(Fig. 4)***.

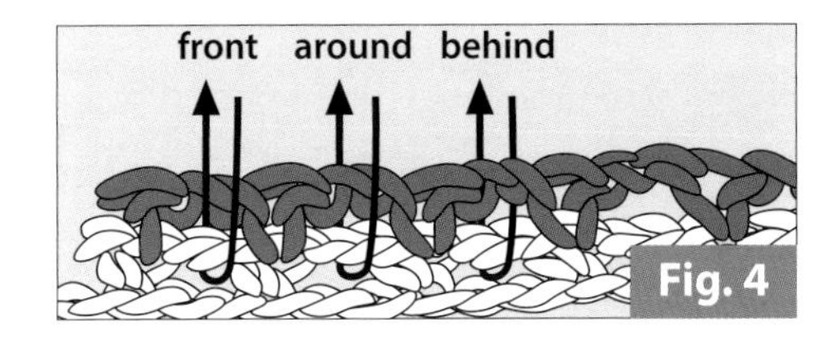

Fig. 4

WORKING IN SPACE BEFORE A STITCH

When instructed to work in space **before** a stitch or in spaces **between** stitches, insert hook in space indicated by arrow ***(Fig. 5)***.

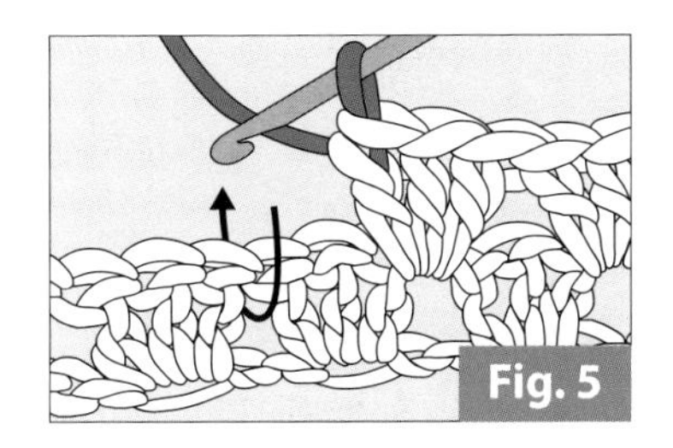

Fig. 5

REVERSE SINGLE CROCHET

(abbreviated reverse sc)

Working from **left** to **right**, ★ insert hook in st to right of hook ***(Fig. 6a)***, YO and draw through, under and to left of loop on hook (2 loops on hook) ***(Fig. 6b)***, YO and draw through both loops on hook ***(Fig. 6c) (reverse sc made, Fig. 6d)***; repeat from ★ around.

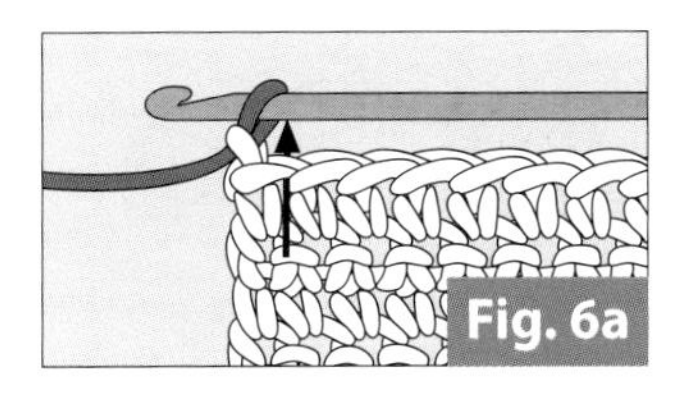

Fig. 6a

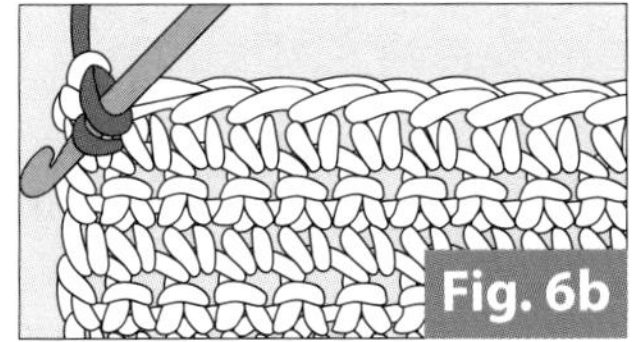

Fig. 6b

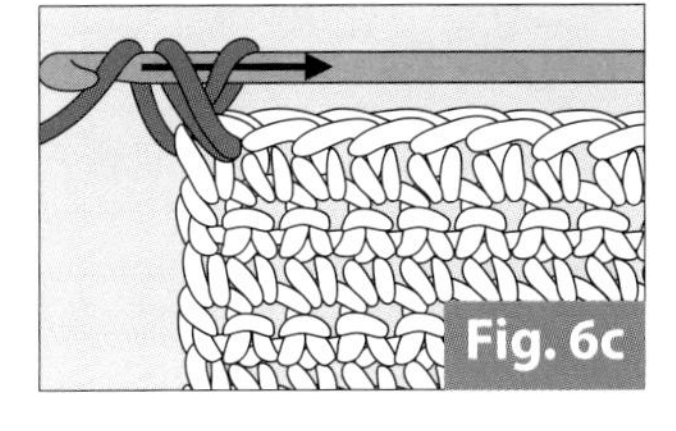

Fig. 6c

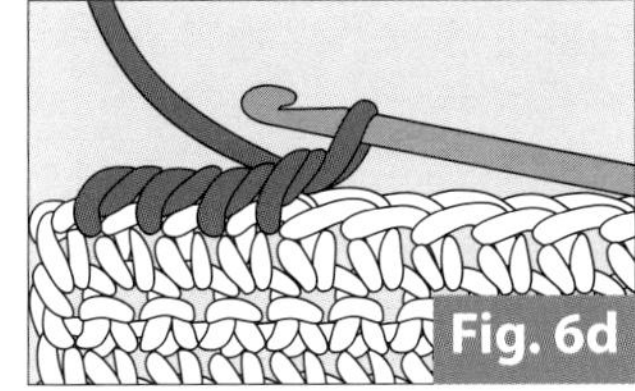

Fig. 6d

REVERSE HALF DOUBLE CROCHET

(abbreviated reverse hdc)

Working from **left** to **right**, YO, insert hook in st or sp indicated to right of hook ***(Fig. 7a)***, YO and draw through, under and to left of loops on hook (3 loops on hook) ***(Fig. 7b)***, YO and draw through all 3 loops on hook ***(Fig. 7c) (reverse hdc made, Fig. 7d)***.

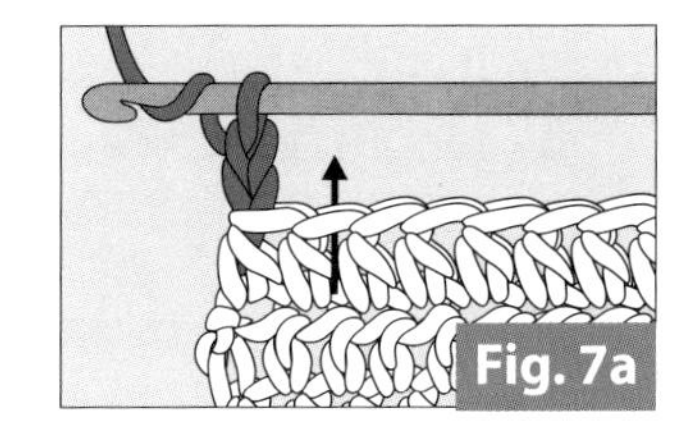

Fig. 7a

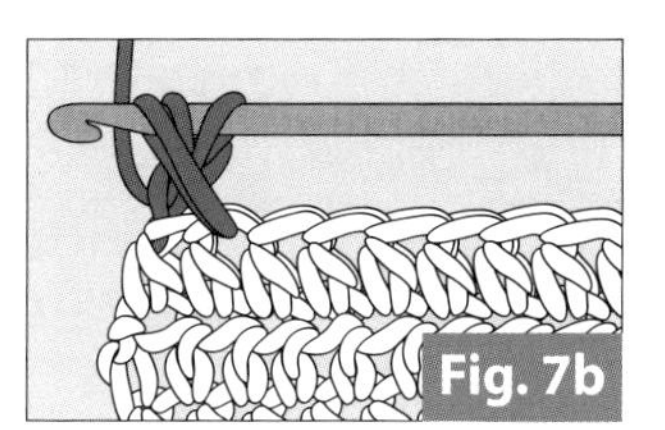

Fig. 7b

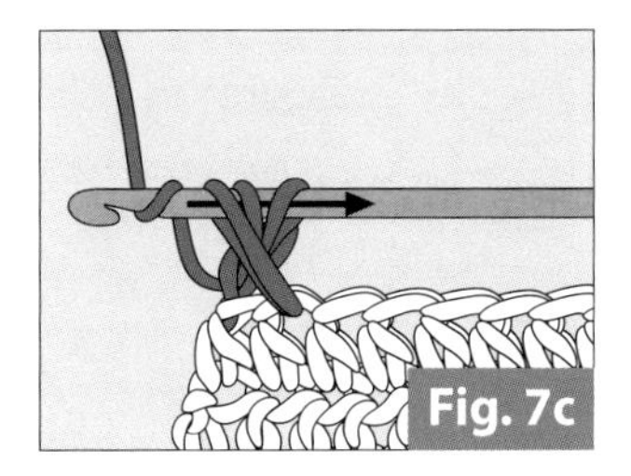

Fig. 7c

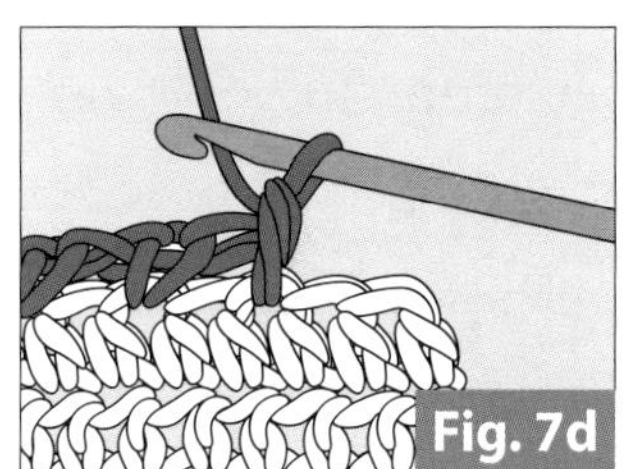

Fig. 7d

WHIPSTITCH

With **wrong** sides together, sew through both pieces once to secure the beginning of the seam. Insert the needle from **right** to **left** through two strands on each piece ***(Fig. 8)***. Bring the needle around and insert it from **right** to **left** through the next strands on both pieces.

Repeat along the edge, being careful to match stitches.

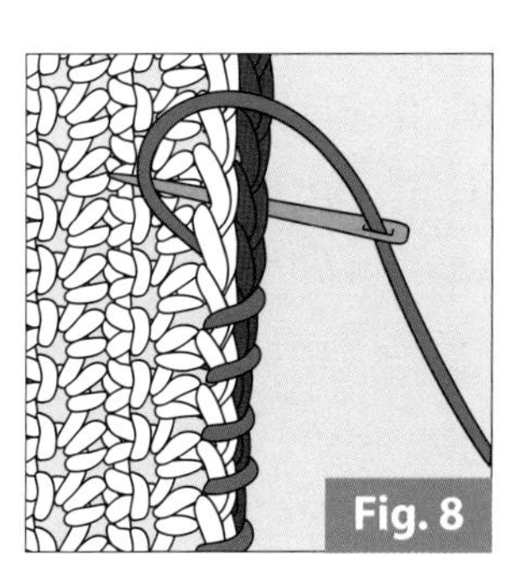

Fig. 8

Yarn Information

Each project in this leaflet was made using Medium Weight Yarn, containing 100% cotton or a blend of cotton. Any brand of Medium Weight Yarn may be used. It is best to refer to the yardage/meters when determining how many balls or skeins to purchase. Remember, to arrive at the finished size, it is the GAUGE/TENSION that is important, not the brand of yarn.

For your convenience, listed below are the yarns used to create our photography models. Because yarn manufacturers make frequent changes in their product lines, you may sometimes find it necessary to use a substitute yarn or to search for the discontinued product at alternate suppliers (locally or online).

OVAL BASKETS
Premier Home™ Cotton
#44-21 Sahara Splash
#38-03 Beige
#38-13 Pastel Blue

BOTTLE CARRIER
Premier Home™ Cotton
#44-17 Fruit Bowl

LACY TOTE
Premier Home™ Cotton
Color A (Green) - #38-15 Sage
Color B (White) - #38-01 White
Color C (Variegated) - #44-17 Fruit Bowl

AIR PLANT HANGER
Lily® Sugar'n Cream®
Color A (Yellow) - #1612 Country Yellow
Color B (Variegated) - #2017 Desert Rising Ombre

BATH SET
Lion Brand® 24/7 Cotton
#143 Lilac
#156 Mint
#158 Goldenrod

COASTER SET
Lily® Sugar'n Cream®
Color A (Variegated) - #2600 Psychedelic Ombre
Color B (Yellow) - #10 Yellow
Color C (Green) - #1223 Mod Green
Color D (Pink) - #1740 Hot Pink

DISHCLOTH & TOWEL
Lily® Sugar'n Cream®
#10 Yellow

POTHOLDER
Lily® Sugar'n Cream®
#2600 Psychedelic Ombre

PLACEMAT SET
Lion Brand® 24/7 Cotton
Main Color (Brown) - #126 Café Au Lait
Color A (Yellow) - #157 Lemon
Color B (Green) - #178 Jade

HALF HEXAGON RUG
Lily® Sugar'n Cream®
Color A (Grey) - #1042 Overcast
Color B (Yellow) - #10 Yellow
Color C (Ecru) - #4 Ecru

We have made every effort to ensure that these instructions are accurate and complete.
We cannot, however, be responsible for human error, typographical mistakes, or variations in individual work.

Items made and instructions tested by Amanda Loggins.

Production Team: Instructional/Technical Editor - Cathy Hardy; Editorial Writer - Susan Frantz Wiles;
Senior Graphic Artist - Lora Puls; Graphic Artist - Kellie McAnulty; Photo Stylist - Lori Wenger; and Photographer - Jason Masters.